GOLF LEGEND

TIGER WOODS

BY DOUG WILLIAMS

Essential Library
An Imprint of Abdo Publishing
abdobooks.com

Published by Abdo Publishing, a division of ABDO, PO Box 398166, Minneapolis, Minnesota 55439. Copyright © 2020 by Abdo Consulting Group, Inc. International copyrights reserved in all countries. No part of this book may be reproduced in any form without written permission from the publisher. Essential Library™ is a trademark and logo of Abdo Publishing.

Printed in the United States of America, North Mankato, Minnesota.
052019
092019

THIS BOOK CONTAINS RECYCLED MATERIALS

Cover Photo: Kyodo/AP Images
Interior Photos: Chris Carlson/AP Images, 4; Kyodo/AP Images, 9, 96; Curtis Compton/Atlanta Journal-Constitution/AP Images, 10; Robert Beck/Icon Sportswire/AP Images, 12, 16; CBS/Getty Images, 14; Bob Galbraith/AP Images, 20, 22; Lennox McLendon/AP Images, 24, 33; David Liam Kyle/Sports Illustrated/Getty Images, 26; Matt York/AP Images, 29; Peter Zuzga/AP Images, 30; Al Messerschmidt/AP Images, 34; Bill Waugh/AP Images, 36; Curtis Compton/AP Images, 39, 43; Amy Sancetta/AP Images, 40, 90; Kunz/AP Images, 44; Beth A. Keiser/AP Images, 46; Charlie Neibergall/AP Images, 49; Adam Butler/AP Images, 54; Damian Dovarganes/AP Images, 56; Michael Conroy/AP Images, 59; Charlie Riedel/AP Images, 61; Chris O'Meara/AP Images, 64; Lynne Cameron/Press Association/AP Images, 66; Jeff Roberson/AP Images, 69; Kathy Willens/AP Images, 71; Joe Skipper/Reuters/AP Images, 72; Tony Bowler/Shutterstock Images, 76; Phelan M. Ebenhack/AP Images, 78; Jim Hunter/Shutterstock Images, 80; AP Images, 83; Keyur Khamar/PGA Tour/Getty Images, 87; Debby Wong/Shutterstock Images, 88; Manuel Balce Ceneta/AP Images, 93

Editor: Patrick Donnelly
Series Designer: Laura Graphenteen

LIBRARY OF CONGRESS CONTROL NUMBER: 2018967305

PUBLISHER'S CATALOGING-IN-PUBLICATION DATA

Names: Williams, Doug, author.
Title: Tiger Woods: golf legend / by Doug Williams
Other title: Golf legend
Description: Minneapolis, Minnesota: Abdo Publishing, 2020 | Series: Star athletes | Includes online resources and index.
Identifiers: ISBN 9781532119927 (lib. bdg.) | ISBN 9781532174759 (ebook) | ISBN 9781644940990 (pbk.)
Subjects: LCSH: Woods, Tiger (Eldrick)--Juvenile literature. | Golfers--United States--Biography--Juvenile literature. | Sports--Biography--Juvenile literature. | African American professional athletes--Biography--Juvenile literature.
Classification: DDC 796.352092 [B]--dc23

CONTENTS

MASTERFUL

Tiger Woods walked onto the green on the eighteenth hole at Augusta National Golf Club, only ten feet between him and a victory that would reclaim his status as the world's greatest golfer.

Woods had been on top of the golf world for a decade. He was the game's best player and its biggest star. Then a series of misfortunes—some self-inflicted, others beyond his control—knocked him from his perch. His longtime fans dreamed of a day when they'd see the old Tiger, the one who intimidated other golfers with his booming tee shots, deadly putting, and unshakable confidence.

But few could have dared hope for *this*. On April 14, 2019, Tiger Woods—at age 43—was putting for the win at the Masters.

LONG ROAD BACK

After a prodigious amateur career, Woods became a household name in 1997 when he won the

Tiger Woods was calm and confident during the final round of the 2019 Masters Tournament.

5

Masters Tournament at age 21. From there, he went on a tear. Woods began piling up victories in golf's four majors—the Masters, the US Open, the British Open, and the PGA Championship—at a record pace. By 2008, he'd collected 14 major titles, and at age 32, Woods appeared to be a lock to break the record of 18, set by the legendary Jack Nicklaus. All the while, Woods's popularity surged, earning him millions of dollars in endorsements while attracting previously unheard of attention to the sport.

But the next decade was a personal and professional disaster for Woods. His marriage dissolved amid a string of infidelities that marred his previously sparkling image. And his body began falling apart. Injuries to his neck, back, left knee, and both Achilles tendons led to multiple surgeries.

Naturally, his play suffered. The man who'd spent more time ranked number one in the world than any player in history watched his ranking plummet to 1,199th by December 2017.

RETURN TO GLORY

Things began to change in 2018, however. A fourth back surgery in April 2017 helped rid him of the pain in his legs and back. And when his health returned, so did his game.

Slowly but surely, Woods inched his way back up the rankings with solid performances on the Professional Golfers' Association (PGA) Tour, including six top-ten finishes. In September, he won the Tour Championship, his first tournament victory in five years. The buzz was unmistakable in the golf world—Tiger was back.

The Masters is the first major on the calendar every year, taking place in early April. Woods had begun 2019 with solid but not spectacular performances in his first five tournaments. But his world ranking had climbed to No. 12, and when the Masters opened, only two players were given better odds to win.

During Thursday's opening round, Woods missed a few makeable putts but avoided

GOLF TERMINOLOGY

Most golf courses have 18 holes, and each of those holes is assigned a score for par, which is the number of shots it should take to complete the hole. Finishing in one shot fewer than expected, or one shot below par—needing only four shots on a par 5 hole, for example—is called a birdie. Two shots below par on a hole is called an eagle. One shot over par for a hole—four shots on a par 3—is a bogey. The total par for most 18-hole courses is 72.

Golfers use a variety of clubs on their journey from tee to green. A wood is used for long-distance shots. A driver is a type of wood with an oversized head and flat face. Most golfers use a driver or another wood when teeing off on a longer hole.

From the fairway, golfers might use a wood or an iron, a shorter club with a slanted metal face that allows them to hit the ball higher in the air. A wedge is the shortest type of iron. It comes in handy close to the green when a player wants a high shot that drops the ball straight down near the hole, reducing its tendency to roll. Finally, a putter is the club golfers use on the green to tap the ball into the hole.

disaster on a windy day. His score of 70, 2 shots under par, left him tied for eleventh place, well within striking range.

Despite two bogeys on the front nine on Friday, Woods managed to rally and finished with a round of 68, 4 shots below par. He also was part of the day's strangest highlight. After hitting his second shot from the rough on No. 14, Woods almost was taken down by a security guard who slipped on the wet grass as he attempted to hold back the spectators. The security guard's knee actually clipped Woods's right ankle, but Tiger walked it off and promptly made a 20-foot putt for birdie. His two-day score of 6 under par was one shot behind a group of five players at 7 under.

On Saturday, an early bogey was the only blemish in an otherwise flawless round. Woods made three straight birdies in the first nine holes and posted three more over four holes of the back nine. The crowd roared as Woods sunk a tricky 7-foot putt on No. 16, in part because his sixth birdie of the day gave him a share of the lead. The day finished with Woods at 11 under for the tournament, two shots behind leader Francesco Molinari, who had surged ahead with two late birdies.

"It's been a while since I've been in contention here," Woods said as he reflected on his third round. "I've got to

Woods, left, just gets out of the way as a security guard takes a tumble in the rough during the second round of the 2019 Masters.

get the mind and body ready for tomorrow and get after it a little earlier than we're used to."[1]

He was referring to an earlier tee time forced by a weather forecast that called for heavy rain on Sunday afternoon. In order to beat the storms, the players were grouped in threesomes rather than the usual pairs and hit the course early on Sunday morning.

The change had little effect on Woods. Leaning on his vast experience in pressure situations, Woods was calm and consistent while others around him struggled.

The crowd ringing the green on No. 18 erupts after Woods closes out his fifth Masters title.

Molinari's third shot on No. 15 splashed into a pond near the green, leading to a double bogey, while Woods drained a short birdie putt to take the lead for the first time at 13 under par.

BRINGING IT HOME

Anyone who doubted that the old Tiger was back had to have been convinced after his tee shot on No. 16. Reading the slope perfectly, Woods dropped an 8-iron to the right of the pin, and the ball rolled to within 4 feet of the hole. He sank the putt for another birdie, increasing his lead to two shots with two holes to play.

None of his competitors could close the gap, so Woods teed off on No. 18 needing a bogey or better to win his fifth Masters title. After a wobbly approach shot, he pitched to within ten feet of the hole. His par putt barely slid past the hole, leaving him a simple tap-in for the championship.

After receiving congratulations from his caddie and playing partners, Woods engulfed his two children in hugs and shared a long embrace with his mother. The scene was reminiscent of his first title, when the first person he embraced was his father and mentor, Earl.

"To have my kids there, it's come full circle," Woods said. "My dad was there in 1997 and now I'm the dad with two kids there."[2]

He also was back on top of the golf world after another amazing performance at the Masters. It hadn't always been easy, and there were a lot of rocky moments along the way. But the world's greatest golfer had completed one of the greatest comeback stories in sports history.

YOUNG TIGER

The little boy came trotting out from behind the curtain, wearing short pants and a red cap. He carried a small red golf bag behind his back. It was October 6, 1978, and Mike Douglas had just introduced two-year-old Tiger Woods to his audience. Douglas hosted *The Mike Douglas Show*, a daytime TV talk show seen coast to coast. Douglas invited Tiger and his dad, Earl Woods, so national television viewers could meet the miniature golf prodigy Douglas had seen on a Los Angeles newscast a few weeks before.

With Douglas and two guests—comedian Bob Hope and actor Jimmy Stewart—standing nearby, Tiger teed up a ball on a patch of plastic grass and took a smooth swing. The ball rocketed off his little driver. Tiger held his pose, just like a pro. The audience members, Hope, Stewart, and Douglas laughed and applauded.

When Hope later challenged Tiger to a putting contest, Tiger missed his first two before

Sixteen-year-old Tiger Woods plays a fairway shot at the 1992 Los Angeles Open, his first pro tournament.

Tiger shows off his form at age two on **The Mike Douglas Show.**

placing the ball next to the hole and tapping in. Hope just laughed.

At age five, Tiger again hit balls on national TV, appearing on ABC's *That's Incredible!* After finishing, he told the host, "When I'm going to be 20, I'm going to beat Jack Nicklaus and Tom Watson."[1]

As time would prove, Tiger didn't just talk a good game. He would grow up to become one of the greatest golfers in history.

HUMBLE BEGINNINGS

Though golf has long been associated in the United States with country clubs and wealth, Tiger's roots were much more modest. The son of a black father and Thai mother, Tiger grew up playing beat-up public courses.

His father, Earl, a former member of the US Army Special Forces, didn't begin playing golf until he was 42. That was just before Earl's fourth child, Eldrick Tont Woods, was born on December 30, 1975, in Cypress, California. Almost from the time he was born, Earl called his son Tiger in honor of a South Vietnamese soldier by that nickname. The soldier had saved Earl's life during the Vietnam War (1954–1975).

Because Earl was so passionate about his new hobby, he'd often hit balls

DAD WAS AROUND, THIS TIME

Earl Woods had three children from a previous marriage. He later said he regretted being an absentee father to his first three children, but he often was away because of his military duty. After he married Kultida, he had retired, so he had more time to spend with Tiger. That meant Tiger got plenty of attention. "Tiger is the only one I've been able to spend his entire life with," said Earl. "The rest of them have big holes. . . . A lot of damage had already been done."[2]

into a net in the garage as Tiger watched from a nearby high chair. After Tiger learned to walk, but before his first birthday, Earl put a club in his son's hands and let him hit a ball in the garage. When the toddler copied what he'd been seeing for months and put a good swing on the ball, Earl ran into the house to tell his wife, Kultida, "We have a genius on our hands."[3]

Though Earl loved the game, he didn't push it on his son. Once Tiger showed he was interested in golf, his father gave him the opportunity to hit balls, play, and get instruction.

"The best thing about those practices was that my father always kept it fun," Tiger once said. "It is amazing how much you can learn when you truly enjoy doing something. Golf for me has always been a labor of love and pleasure."[4]

Tiger took his first lessons at a little par-3 course in Long Beach, California, when he was four years old. He practiced hitting, chipping, and putting all morning, ate lunch, and then played in the afternoon, usually accompanied by his mother. Before he was five, he made

Earl Woods was a driving force in Tiger's career.

his first birdie—on a 91-yard par-3. However, he lost his match that day to his mother, who shot 66 to his 70.

Even before Tiger took his first lesson, golf pro Rudy Duran said the four-year-old knew exactly what to do. His clubface always was in perfect position and his swing was fundamentally sound and the same every time. "I felt he was like Mozart," said Duran.[5]

FIRST CHAMPIONSHIPS

In 1984, eight-year-old Tiger won his first trophy at the annual Junior World Golf Championships in San Diego, California. The tournament, started in 1968, was a magnet for the best junior players from around the country and world. Future professional stars such as Craig Stadler, Nick Price, Amy Alcott, and Phil Mickelson had won age-group championships there before Tiger made his first appearance.

Tiger—who at the time wore big, thick glasses—won the ten-and-under age division on a par-3 course, beating future PGA Tour player Chris Riley by two shots. At the time, Riley was ten. "He had the Coke-bottle thick glasses, but he could flat-out play," recalled Riley years later.[6] The win was the first of what would be a record six age-group Junior World titles for Tiger.

As Tiger grew, his passion for the game went beyond playing. He loved golf's history and stars and dreamed of winning big tournaments such as the Masters and the US Open. In his bedroom hung a poster of Jack Nicklaus and a list of Nicklaus's 18 major golf championships as a goal to surpass.

Tiger and Earl loved to play together. They were not only father and son but good friends. In 1987, about a month before he turned 12, Tiger beat his father for the first time, by one shot, while playing on a course in Long Beach.

Tiger's mother was equally influential. It was she who most often drove Tiger to practices and tournaments, and it was she who instilled discipline in him. She was loving but demanding.

"People say that Tiger had natural ability, that God gave him the ability to play golf. No. God gave him a work ethic, and he put that work ethic to good use. Even at a young age, he was the hardest worker I'd ever seen." [8]
— *Don Crosby, Tiger's coach at Western High in Anaheim, California.*

"As we said in our family, my mom was the hand and my dad was the voice," recalled Tiger years later. "I could negotiate with him, but not with my mom. There was no middle ground with mom."[7]

As a young golfer, Tiger stood out both for his talent and his race.

By the time Tiger was 14, he was playing in youth tournaments across the United States. When he traveled, he occasionally encountered racism. Some people were uncomfortable with a young mixed-race player competing or even practicing at venues where white players and members were the norm.

"Every time I go to a major country club, I can always feel it, can always sense it," he said at 14. "People always staring at you. 'What are you doing here? You shouldn't be here.' When you go to Texas, go to Florida, you always feel it."[9]

NATIONAL SENSATION

At 16, Tiger received a special invitation to play in his first PGA Tour event, the 1992 Nissan Los Angeles Open at the famed Riviera Country Club. Just a sophomore in high school, he was skinny at about 140 pounds (64 kg), but he was six feet one (185 cm) and could hit the ball more than 300 yards.

Some pros weren't happy with the invitation, believing Tiger didn't belong on the course with golf's best players. But Tiger drew big crowds and impressed the pros. He birdied his very first hole in Round 1 and shot a 1-over-par 72. He followed with a 4-over 75 in Round 2 to miss the cut.

TIGER SCARED DALY

At 13, Tiger Woods played in the 1989 National Insurance Youth Golf Classic in Texarkana, Texas, an event that paired promising young amateurs with professionals. Woods was only 5 feet 5 (165 cm) and weighed just over 100 pounds (45 kg), but he gave pro John Daly a scare. Woods was 3 under par over the first nine holes, four shots better than Daly. "I can't let a 13-year-old beat me," said Daly, then 23.[10] He then rallied on the back nine to finish two shots better than Woods.

Tiger—at age 17—reacts after making a birdie putt at the 1993 Los Angeles Open, his second appearance in the tournament.

"It was a learning experience," he said. "And I learned that I wasn't that good."[11]

Tiger was invited to participate in six other PGA Tour events while in high school. He missed the cut in all. Perhaps he wasn't yet ready for the pro tour, but as an amateur he was a star. In 1991 at age 15, he became the youngest player at the time to win the US Golf Association's Junior Amateur championship. Then he won it again in 1992 and 1993. Still a senior in high school, Tiger was two holes down with two holes to play in the match play format in 1993. But he won the last two holes to force a playoff. He then beat his opponent, Ryan Armour, on the first extra hole.

"I don't think many people could have done what Tiger did—professional, amateur, junior amateur, whatever," said Armour. "That's why he's the best."[12]

On the course that day, too, were coaches from Stanford, Arizona State, and the University of Nevada, Las Vegas (UNLV), the three schools vying for Tiger to play college golf. He was more than ready to take his game to the next level.

NEVER, EVER QUIT

Once, while playing in a youth tournament in Miami, Tiger lost a lead, fell behind, and essentially quit. Earl Woods said his son "threw away a few strokes" and gave away any chance of winning. Afterward, Earl confronted Tiger privately, telling him he should never, ever stop trying. "Who do you think you are? How dare you not try your best," said Earl. "You embarrassed yourself and you shamed me."[13] Earl said he never saw Tiger quit again.

INVITATIONAL
Oc
Tiger Woods
ndred Ninety Seven Thousand and 00
OF AMERICA
Tourname

"HELLO, WORLD"

T iger Woods agonized about where to go to college. After narrowing his list to Stanford and UNLV, he put so much pressure on himself to make the right choice that he became physically ill.

Finally, on November 10, 1993, the 17-year-old golfer announced he would attend Stanford. He chose the university in Palo Alto, California, not only for its fine golf program but also for its academic excellence. Woods's parents had always stressed the importance of an education, and his grade point average in high school was better than 3.7. Stanford even promised to create a major just for him, tailored to his desire to focus on business and accounting.

"It came down to what school I would become a better person at," said Woods. "I figured, what's more important, school or golf? My entire life has always been about school first, golf second, so why change now?"[1]

A 20-year-old Tiger Woods smiles after winning his first tournament as a professional.

Woods and his Stanford teammate Casey Martin hang out at a tournament in 1995.

At Stanford, Woods would play for coach Wally Goodwin, who led Stanford to the National Collegiate Athletic Association (NCAA) championship in the spring of 1994. When Woods arrived that fall as a freshman, he joined a talented group that included future PGA Tour players Notah Begay III and Casey Martin. Other team members were Will Yanagisawa, who posted the third-lowest score at the 1994 NCAA Championship, and Steve Burdick, known as the team's best overall player.

Instantly, Woods's new teammates could see how good he was. Martin said Woods was the best clutch putter he'd ever seen, and Burdick said, "he had more game than any of us." When Burdick asked Woods what he did besides golf, Woods said, "Eat and sleep."[2] But it was Begay, a few years older and a longtime friend from junior golf, who helped Woods relax. Begay treated him like just another freshman and joked with Woods about his relatively nerdy personality.

DOMINANT AMATEUR

On the course, Woods's closeness with his teammates paid off. In his first season he helped Stanford reach the NCAA final, which it lost to Oklahoma State. He was ranked second in the nation as a freshman. In 1996, Woods won the conference and NCAA individual championships as Stanford finished fourth in the country. Woods was named the national player of the year as a sophomore. In two collegiate seasons, he won 11 of the 26 tournaments he entered.

Meanwhile, Woods continued to dominate amateur golf. The summer before he started at Stanford, he won

MASTERS DEBUT

As the defending US Amateur champion, Woods qualified to play at the 1995 Masters. He shot even-par 72s the first two rounds. He was 5-over on Saturday and shot even-par again on Sunday to finish at 5-over for the tournament, far behind the leaders. For one round Woods was paired with Hall of Famer Gary Player, who marveled at the 19-year-old's skill.

"I thought, man, this young guy has got it," said Player. After the tournament, Woods wrote a letter of thanks to Augusta National, saying his week at the Masters "was Fantasyland and Disney World wrapped into one."[3]

the US Amateur championship at 18, the youngest player ever to win it. He won it again in 1995 and then became the first to win three in a row by going two extra holes to beat Steve Scott on the thirty-eighth hole of match play in August 1996. It was his sixth consecutive national amateur championship, but it would also be his last. He'd already decided to turn pro after the event.

When Woods entered Stanford, he planned to attend four years, graduate, and then turn professional. But in his two years at Stanford, his game had improved more quickly than he expected. Plus, he'd gained experience playing against pros in events such as the British Open and the Masters, for which he qualified as US Amateur champion in 1995 and 1996. When he shot a round of 5-under-par 66 in the second round of the British Open that July, he said he began to seriously think about

Woods embraces his father after winning the US Amateur championship in 1995.

turning pro. He knew he could compete against the best in the world.

"Something really clicked that day, like I had found a whole new style of playing," he said. "I finally understood the meaning of playing within myself. Ever since, the game has seemed a lot easier."[4]

Woods answers questions at a press conference the day after he announced he was turning pro at the 1996 Greater Milwaukee Open.

CASHING IN

Also, by turning pro, Woods was about to become a multimillionaire. Two days after winning the US Amateur, Woods released a statement saying he was turning pro in time to play in the PGA Tour's Greater Milwaukee Open that week. After flying to Milwaukee with Nike executive Phil Knight, Woods held a news conference on August 28 to make the official announcement. He would play Round 1 the next day as a pro. He appeared at the news conference wearing Nike apparel, and his first words that day were, "I guess, hello, world."[5]

It was part of Nike's new marketing campaign for Woods, who had just signed a $40 million, five-year endorsement deal with the company.[6] Nike launched an advertising campaign that weekend on network television and in national newspapers. It was called "Hello, World," and it introduced Woods to sports fans as golf's new star and the latest member of its endorsement team. Woods also signed a five-year deal with golf-equipment manufacturer Titleist worth $20 million.[7]

Woods's presence drew large galleries for the tournament, even though his first pro start wasn't awe inspiring. He shot 7 under par over four rounds in Milwaukee. That gave him a tie for sixtieth place and $2,544 in winnings. His highlight came in the fourth

"The number one player in the world isn't getting that kind of money. Here's a guy who hasn't got his tour card yet."[8]

— PGA Tour pro Steve Stricker, on the resentment some people on tour felt that Woods in 1996 received huge endorsement deals before ever playing an event as a professional

CONTROVERSIAL CAMPAIGN

Nike's "Hello, World" TV ad for Woods in 1996 was attention grabbing and controversial because it made his race part of its campaign. This was the script:

"I shot in the 70s when I was eight. I shot in the 60s when I was 12. I played in the Nissan Open when I was 16. Hello, world. I won the US Amateur when I was 18. I played in the Masters when I was 19. I am the only man to win three consecutive US Amateur titles. Hello, world. There are still courses in the US I am not allowed to play because of the color of my skin. Hello, world. I've heard I'm not ready for you. Are you ready for me?"[9]

Some criticized the campaign as inaccurate, including one *Washington Post* columnist who got Nike to concede there actually were no courses at the time that would refuse to allow a three-time US Amateur champion to play. Managers of some courses were so upset that they refused to sell Nike products.

round, when he made a hole in one.

Though he joined the 1996 PGA Tour far into its season, Woods hoped to play well enough over the final weeks to finish among the season's top 125 money earners. That would qualify him to be a full-time tour player in 1997. Also, a win in any event would automatically qualify him for all tour events for the next two years.

FIRST VICTORY

Over the next three weeks, Woods finished eleventh at the Bell Canadian Open, tied for fifth at the Quad City Classic, and tied for third at the B. C. Open. Two weeks later, in the five-round Las Vegas Invitational, the 20-year-old rookie gave the fans something to remember by shooting a

Davis Love III, right, congratulates Woods for winning the sudden death playoff at the 1996 Las Vegas Invitational.

final-round 64 to tie veteran Davis Love III for the lead. He then beat Love in a sudden-death playoff to earn the $297,000 winner's check.

"We've got to get used to it," Love said after losing to Woods. "I think everybody had better watch out. He's going to be a force."[10]

When Woods was asked whether he was surprised to win so quickly, in just his fifth pro start, he said, "To be honest, I'm surprised it took this long."[11]

Woods signs autographs at the J. C. Penney Classic in November 1996.

Woods played three more PGA Tour events that year, finishing third at the LaCantera Texas Open and winning the Walt Disney World/Oldsmobile Classic in Orlando, Florida, earning $216,000. He then finished his year with a tie for twenty-first in the Tour Championship.

His presence in Orlando attracted a large gallery every day, a diverse group of fans that included many African Americans. "They used to say this was a white man's sport," said one black woman from Georgia who made the trip just to see Woods. "Well, not anymore. They used to say it was boring, too. But not with all the money this young man is making."[12]

Woods was selected PGA Tour Rookie of the Year and had earned more than $790,000, good for twenty-fourth on the money list, giving him PGA Tour playing privileges. He also showed he was a force. He averaged more than 302 yards per drive, topping the 288.8 yards of John Daly, the official leader for the season, as Woods hadn't played enough to qualify. His scoring average of 69.443 would have ranked second to Tom Lehman's 69.321 if he had qualified. *Sports Illustrated* selected Woods as its Sports Person of the Year.

As 1996 came to a close, Woods turned 21 on December 30. The golf world was eager to see what he could accomplish in a full year as a professional in 1997.

HELPING OTHERS

After he turned pro in 1996, Woods and his father started the Tiger Woods Foundation. The nonprofit aimed to raise and distribute money to help kids, especially those in underrepresented communities, get better access to educational opportunities. Since it was founded, the foundation has turned its focus to helping boys and girls succeed in STEM (science, technology, engineering and math) programs through Tiger Woods Learning Centers across the country. In 2018, the name of the foundation was changed to the TGR Foundation.

SUPERSTAR

Tiger Woods had the lead, but he still had a long way to go. Two rounds of the 1997 Masters Tournament were complete, and the 21-year-old Woods was taking Georgia's Augusta National Golf Club by storm. He had a three-stroke lead in his first major tournament as a professional.

Yet the Masters can be cruel. Its slick greens, plentiful water hazards, and sloping fairways are treacherous. One wayward shot can cost a player a chance to win the coveted green jacket awarded to every champion.

People were excited to see Woods play in the tournament. At a lean six feet one (185 cm), he could hit the ball farther than any player on tour, and he played with a maturity beyond his years. In 1996, the great Jack Nicklaus predicted Woods might win more than ten Masters titles.[1]

The prospect of Woods winning at Augusta, where black players hadn't even been allowed to participate until 1975, made this Masters a

Tiger Woods holds the winner's trophy after blowing away the competition at the 1997 Masters Tournament.

particularly compelling tournament. Oddsmakers had made Woods a cofavorite to win.

ROCKY BEGINNING

Woods started slow with a 4-over-par 40 on the first nine holes of his first round on Thursday. But after identifying and correcting a swing flaw on the way to the tenth tee, Woods rallied to finish just three strokes behind the leader. Then in the second round Friday, Woods shot a 6-under-par 66 to take the lead. He was brilliant, but he knew he had to stay focused.

As the leader, Woods had to wait until after 2:00 p.m. to tee off on Saturday. Woods spent part of that time getting a pep talk from his father. Earl's message was simple: "Kick some butt."[2]

The third round of a tournament is known as "moving day" because it's a chance for players to make their move going into the final round. On this day, Woods kept moving forward while those chasing him fell back.

Woods birdied the second hole to take a five-shot lead. Woods birdied three more holes on the front nine.

GREAT RATINGS

Even nongolf fans were captivated by Tiger Woods's Masters victory in 1997. An estimated 44 million people tuned in to watch Woods win his first green jacket.[3] The final round was the highest-rated Masters round of all time.

Woods was just 21 years old when he took the golf world by storm in 1997.

He then did the same at No. 11 and No. 15. Finally, he tapped in a 1-foot birdie putt on No. 18 to finish his day. His 7-under-par 65 put him at 15 under par, tying the tournament record for lowest score after three rounds. The closest golfer to Woods was Italy's Costantino Rocca at 6 under par. Woods would go into Sunday with a nine-stroke lead, the largest advantage held after the third round of any major tournament since 1934.

Kultida Woods, Tiger's mother, enjoys a moment with Nike executive Phil Knight after the third round of the 1997 Masters.

Woods was like a machine. Only one of his tee shots missed the fairway all day. He reached the green in regulation—meaning he had a chance to make birdie with one putt—on all but one hole. He didn't have a single bogey. He had taken his father's advice and tripled his lead.

LIFELONG GOAL

This was the tournament he'd always dreamed of winning. Of the four major tournaments in men's professional golf, the Masters had always been Woods's favorite. He'd been talking about winning it since he was five years old. Late that Saturday night, on the eve of what could be his first Masters win, Woods and his father sat together to eat ice cream and talk about the next day.

Earl gave Tiger some simple advice that night. "Son, this will probably be one of your toughest rounds of golf you've ever had to play in your life," Tiger recalled Earl saying. "Just go out there and be yourself, and it will be one of the most rewarding rounds you've ever played in your life."[4]

Before he teed off the next day, Woods met Lee Elder, who broke the color barrier at the Masters in 1975. That morning Elder and his wife had flown from their home in Florida to Atlanta and rented a car to drive to Augusta, just to wish Woods well.

"I made history here, and I came here today to see more history made," Elder said.

"The 1997 Masters wasn't so much a 'Hello, world' moment. It was more like, 'Watch out, world.'"[5]
— Rival golfer David Duval on Woods's feat

DISTANCE MATTERS

In winning the 1997 Masters, Tiger Woods averaged 323.1 yards in driving distance, 25 yards better than the next-longest golfer. He also averaged just 29 putts per 18 holes on the fast Augusta National greens and never needed more than two putts on any hole.

His length was crucial in dominating the long par-5 holes because he could hit more accurate, shorter irons into greens than other players. While he was even par on the par-3 holes, he was 5 under par on the par 4s and 13 under on the par 5s, with two eagles.

"After today, no one will turn their head when a black man walks to the first tee."[5]

BRINGING IT HOME

Woods had a birdie and two bogeys among his first seven holes. But he then got into a groove with a birdie on No. 8 and three more on Nos. 11, 13, and 14. His 3-under-par 69 in the final round gave him the record score of 18-under 270, beating runner-up Tom Kite by 12 strokes. He also was the youngest Masters champion.

Woods, with a giant smile, punched the air with a big uppercut. Then he walked to the edge of the green to embrace his father. His eyes filled with tears as the two hugged for several moments. "We made it," said Earl. "We made it. We made it."[7]

Woods had dominated the greatest golfers in the world and one of golf's iconic courses. And he made it look easy.

Woods celebrates after closing out his first Masters title with a par putt on the final hole.

At the victory presentation, Woods was presented with his trophy and the green jacket. He slipped it on and beamed. Earl Woods was a proud father, taking it all in. "Green and black go well together, don't they?" he said.[8] Golf had a new superstar.

CHARGING AHEAD

For the golf world, 1997 was the year of Tiger Woods. After dominating the Masters in April, in June he became the youngest golfer ever, at 21, to be ranked number one in the world. He won four times on the PGA Tour and earned more than $2 million to lead the money list.

Yet Woods took a step back in 1998. For almost any other player, his second full year on tour would have been good. He won one tournament, finished in the top three in four others, and earned $1.8 million. But more was expected after 1997. In 1998, he didn't meet those expectations. He was just a little off. His shots weren't as consistently on target as the year before. However, there was a reason.

Woods and his coach, Butch Harmon, had made some changes to his swing, which Woods continued to work on while he played. While

Tiger Woods began dominating the PGA Tour after his 1997 Masters victory.

Butch Harmon helps Woods refine his swing on the driving range at the 1999 PGA Championship.

Woods's swing had been good enough to win and sometimes dominate, Woods and Harmon believed he needed to shorten his swing. They thought it would give him more accuracy for golf's toughest tournaments, such as the US Open and British Open. Those events feature tighter fairways and nasty rough, making accuracy even more important. That meant taking a couple of steps back in 1998 to take three steps forward in 1999 and beyond.

"Your golf swing is not always going to be good," said Woods. "You can always work on it, and hopefully it will evolve to where it's good again."[1]

SCALING BACK

Being constantly in the public eye can be exhausting. One way Woods learned to relax was by fishing. His friend and fellow pro golfer Mark O'Meara introduced Woods to fly fishing in 1997, and Woods has fished all over the country, from Florida to Alaska. He says one reason he likes to fish is, "Fish don't ask for autographs."[2]

TIGER SLAM

Starting in 1999, Woods was locked in with his new swing. From 1999 through 2002, Woods won seven major championships: two Masters, two US Opens, two PGA Championships, and one British Open. Over those four years he won 27 PGA Tour events and was named PGA Tour Player of the Year four times. In 2000, he was again *Sports Illustrated*'s Sports Person of the Year.

His greatest achievement was winning four consecutive majors. Winning all four in a single year is called the Grand Slam, a feat no player has accomplished since 1930, when the four majors were different than they are today. When Woods won the US Open, British Open, and PGA Championship in 2000, then won the first major of 2001, the Masters, he held title to all four modern majors at once, something that had never been done. It became known as the "Tiger Slam."

Woods's special feat began with a record 15-stroke victory at the US Open at Pebble Beach, California, in June. While his competitors struggled with the wind and challenging layout, Woods wasn't fazed. He finished a record 12 strokes under par for the four rounds. After his win, former US Open champion Tom Watson said, "Tiger has raised the bar, and it seems that he's the only guy who can jump over that bar."[3]

A month later, Woods won the British Open at the famous Old Course at Saint Andrew's, Scotland, by shooting 19 under par and winning by eight strokes. That gave him a career grand slam (wins in all four majors, but not necessarily in the same year) by age 24, two years earlier than Jack Nicklaus had done it.

Woods's third major victory in a row wasn't as easy. He and Bob May were paired in the final round of the PGA Championship and dueled all day. They finished tied for the lead at 18 under par to tie the tournament record. That sent it to a three-hole playoff, which Woods won by a shot.

Woods had to wait eight months for the Masters to complete the slam. He came in hot, having won two

Woods hoists the Wanamaker Trophy, awarded to the PGA Championship winner, after he edged Bob May in a playoff in 2000.

straight tournaments that year. But he had to fight at Augusta National, fending off challenges from David Duval and Phil Mickelson. He beat Duval by two strokes, closing with a flourish by sinking an 18-foot putt for a birdie on the final hole. When the ball dropped in, he pumped his fist in triumph. Later, he had tears in his eyes

COURSES ARE "TIGER-PROOFED"

After Woods's win at the Masters in 1997, many courses, including Augusta National, were lengthened. The theory was that Woods hit the ball so far that he had an unfair advantage. Plus, Woods's record-setting scores were embarrassing for courses that had the reputation of being difficult. Because Woods hit the ball farther off the tee, he was able to hit shorter irons into greens than his opponents. Shorter irons—such as a 9-iron instead of a 6-iron—allow for a higher shot, so the ball lands and stays closer to the hole. The Masters added about 300 yards to its layout by 2002 and is now 500 yards longer than it was in 1997. Other tournaments such as the annual US Open also were lengthened. But "Tiger-proofing," as it was called, actually gave Woods an advantage, because it nearly eliminated the chances of shorter hitters posting low scores.

as he talked about what he'd just accomplished. "I've never had that feeling before," he said.[4]

At the awards ceremony, Augusta National chair Hootie Johnson said, "We have witnessed the greatest golfing feat of our time."[5] Added Woods: "Some of the golfing gods are looking down on me the right way."[6]

At 25, Woods had won his sixth major tournament and had his twenty-seventh win in 98 tour events. He had led 13 of the 16 rounds over the four majors.

THE PEOPLE'S CHAMPION

Along with dominating on the golf course, Woods's charisma and animated, athletic style of play continued to draw more viewers to TVs, fans to PGA Tour events, and money from sponsorships. It was known as "the Tiger Effect."

When Woods won the 2001 Masters, the final-round TV ratings were the second highest in tournament history, with more than 40 million viewers.[7] That number was just four million fewer than the record number who watched Tiger win his first Masters in 1997. Throughout Woods's quest for the four straight championships, TV ratings rose to record levels. Since he turned pro, Woods had become a TV star. When he played, ratings soared. If he didn't, ratings suffered.

Golf had long been considered by many to be a boring sport that appealed only to the white upper class. But Woods made golf cool. By the time he won the Tiger Slam, celebrities and icons from other sports, such as basketball star Michael Jordan, were playing the game, talking about it, and in some cases, hanging out with Woods.

"Tiger embodied a kind of modern cool that golf hadn't seen before," said Orin Starn, a professor at Duke University who wrote the book *The Passion of Tiger Woods*. Starn said Woods was a "charismatic, young African-American-Asian-American hybrid figure" who burst onto a pro tour of players "who mostly looked and dressed alike," so it was no wonder Woods drew more TV

RYDER CUP SUCCESS

Since 1927, one of the biggest competitions in golf has been the Ryder Cup. Every two years, a team of US golfers takes on a team from Europe. Woods first played in the Cup in 1997, but he went just 1–3–1 in his five matches. Though his career Ryder Cup record is a disappointing 13–21–3, two of his victories came in 1999 when the United States beat Europe by just a point. Included was a final-day singles victory over Andrew Coltart of Scotland that gave the US team its first lead of the competition. It would be the only time Woods was part of a winning US Ryder Cup team.

viewers and larger galleries.[8] Plus, the tour and Woods's sponsors marketed him as a must-see athlete. After the Tiger Slam, a poll of American fans named him the nation's number-one athlete.[9] Not a basketball player, not a football star, not an Olympian—a golfer.

On-course attendance also surged with Tiger. In 1996, the average attendance at a four-day PGA Tour event was about 106,000. By 1999, it was 148,809, an increase of more than 28 percent. Average ticket revenue increased more than 48 percent during that same span.[10] Many of those tickets were sold to people who didn't know much about the game except that Woods was in town.

One element of his charisma was his athleticism. Woods became a fitness fanatic. He lifted weights and put on 30 pounds (14 kg) of muscle. He was dedicated to winning, and fitness was a part of the formula. In order to keep up with him, other golfers including Duval and later

Rory McIlroy and Jason Day followed his example. PGA Tour player Chris Riley said golfers suddenly weren't going out for beers after a round anymore. Instead, they were working out with personal trainers.

Meanwhile, as Woods was winning tournaments and majors, he and other golfers were making more money. Woods's presence on tour attracted more sponsors and allowed the tour to negotiate more lucrative deals with TV networks. In 1996, the PGA Tour awarded $101 million in prize money. By 2008, that total had nearly tripled to $292 million. Mickelson, who was perhaps Woods's strongest rival over his career, said he and every other golfer owe much to Woods.

"Tiger has been the instigator," said Mickelson. "He's been the one that's really propelled and driven the bus because he's brought increased ratings, increased sponsors, increased interest, and we have all benefited."[11]

HUSBAND, FATHER, CHAMPION

As 2008 began, Woods was riding high, both on and off the course. At 32, Woods had been the top-ranked golfer in the world since June 2005. After beginning the 2008 season with a win at the Buick Invitational at Torrey Pines in San Diego, he had 62 career victories. He was now tied for fourth in all-time wins with Arnold Palmer. He also had 13 major championships, just five behind Jack Nicklaus's record of 18. And Nicklaus hadn't won his thirteenth major until he was 35. Since completing the Tiger Slam in 2001, Woods had been the PGA Tour's Player of the Year every season but one.

Plus, Woods seemed like the happiest of family men now. Though he lost his father, Earl, to cancer in 2006, Woods now had a wife and child. He married Elin Nordegren, a former model from

Tiger Woods and his then girlfriend, Elin Nordegren, attend the opening ceremony for the Ryder Cup in 2002.

Woods and his family—daughter Sam Alexis, mother Kultida, and wife Elin—stand in front of a statue of Tiger and Earl Woods at the Tiger Woods Learning Center in 2008.

Sweden, in 2004. Their daughter, Sam Alexis, was born in June 2007.

When Woods won the PGA Championship two months later, it was his first major title as a dad. He said it was emotional to have his family with him. Just like her father, who always wears a red shirt on the final day of a tournament, little Sam was decked out in red for the fourth round that day.

"It used to be my mom and dad," Woods said at the victory ceremony. "And now Elin, and now we have our own daughter. So it's evolved, and this one feels so much more special than the other majors."[1]

READY TO DOMINATE

Now, at the start of a new year, Woods was eager and confident. He'd won seven times in 2007, and the January 2008 victory at Torrey Pines was his sixth there as a pro. Torrey Pines would be the site of the US Open that June, so if a major was ever tailor-made for him, it would be this one. After winning at Torrey Pines in January by a record eight strokes, his fourth in a row on the course, he said he was playing at the highest level of his career. The win in San Diego gave him three straight PGA Tour wins, dating to 2007, by a combined 18 shots. Many of his fellow tour

STAR-STUDDED WEDDING

Of course, Woods's wedding to Elin Nordegren took place near a golf course. Golfer Jesper Parnevik introduced Woods to Nordegren, who was working as his nanny. The couple was married on October 5, 2004, at a country club in Barbados. Guests included family, friends, and celebrities such as basketball stars Michael Jordan and Charles Barkley, Microsoft founder Bill Gates, and multimedia giant Oprah Winfrey. Woods spent more than $1.5 million to rent out the entire country club to ensure privacy.[2] At the time of the wedding, Woods's worth was estimated at $370 million.[3]

A HUGE LOSS

It was a huge blow to Woods when his father, Earl, died in May 2006. In the early years of his son's pro career, Earl was often there alongside the green when Tiger had his greatest victories. "My dad was my best friend and greatest role model," Woods said at the time of his father's death. "He was an amazing dad, coach, mentor, soldier, husband, and friend." Earl said he never treated his son like a kid but as an equal. "We transcended the parent-child relationship and became best friends a long time ago," he said.[4] Woods once wrote he always appreciated how his father and mother raised him, saying their role was "one of support and guidance, not interference."[5]

pros said they'd never seen him better.

Woods had rebounded from a slight slump over the 2003 and 2004 seasons, when he didn't win a major. In 2004, he changed swing coaches, from Butch Harmon to Hank Haney, and again it took him a while to feel comfortable and confident. Woods, always the perfectionist, went to Haney to improve on what already was the winningest swing in golf, so some observers were baffled by the move. But Woods and Haney tweaked the swing to take pressure off Woods's left knee, which had bothered him for several years.

Now, with confidence and a winning streak, Woods followed up his Buick victory with wins in his next two tournaments. Then, in April, Woods finished second at the Masters. Two days later, his season and career took an unexpected turn.

Woods and Hank Haney discuss strategy at the 2006 US Open at New York's Winged Foot Golf Club.

KNEE PROBLEMS

On April 15, Woods entered Healthsouth Surgical Center in Park City, Utah. He was there for what he thought would be a simple arthroscopic surgery on his left knee to repair some cartilage damage. He expected to be back playing within weeks. But during the procedure, the doctor discovered Woods also had a ruptured anterior cruciate ligament (ACL). Woods was advised to have ACL reconstruction surgery, but he opted to put it off till the end of the year so he could play the major tournaments.

Then, while on the course for a photo shoot, Woods suffered two fractures of his left tibia, the primary bone extending from the knee to ankle. Doctors told him he was done for the year. Woods, however, rejected their advice. He would delay surgery and continue to play.

"Tiger looks up and says, 'I'm playing in the US Open and I'm going to win,'" said Haney, his coach. "Just like that. Then he says, 'C'mon, Hank. Let's go practice.' The determination was absolutely incredible."[6]

Over the coming weeks, Woods tried wearing a brace on his knee, but he discarded it because it was too bulky. Eventually, he decided he could cut back on his practice and learn to play through the pain.

"I thought maybe I could play the US Open and then rest it and then play the British and then play the PGA and just skip all the other tournaments in between," said Woods.[7]

Woods grimaces and holds his aching knee during the third round of the 2008 US Open at Torrey Pines.

GRITTING IT OUT

When it came time to play the Open at Torrey Pines in June, Woods was there. He hadn't played since the Masters, and nobody outside his inner circle knew the severity of his injury. But during the first round, it was apparent Woods was hurt. After hitting his tee shots, he often bent over in pain.

"Watching Tiger on Thursday, I was first amazed that he finished the round," said Jim Vernon, president of the US Golf Association, who walked with Woods's group that day. "Second, I was amazed he came back Friday to play. I couldn't believe how much pain he was in and how much he subjected his body to."[8]

Woods shot a 1-over-par 72 in the first round and a 3-under 68 on the second day to tie for second place, one shot behind the leader. The South Course at Torrey Pines was one of the longest US Open courses at more than 7,600 yards, with thick rough and a challenging design, but even a damaged Woods was taming it.

On the third day, however, Woods stumbled. He made a double bogey on the first hole and added two bogeys through No. 12 to fall three strokes behind leader Rocco Mediate. Then, suddenly, Woods locked in. Over the final six holes he had a birdie and two eagles and three fist-pumping celebrations. When he sank a 60-foot downhill putt for an eagle on No. 18, he had a round of 1-under 70. The score gave him the lead at 3 under, one stroke better than Lee Westwood and two better than Mediate.

HEAD TO HEAD

The fourth round on Sunday was a duel between Woods and Mediate. Mediate, playing one group ahead of Woods, took an early lead before Woods took it back with birdies on No. 9 and No. 11. But Woods made bogeys on Nos. 13 and 15 to give Mediate the lead again. When Woods, still limping and feeling pain, teed up his ball on No. 18, he trailed Mediate by a shot. It appeared his magic had run out. He hooked his tee shot into a fairway bunker and followed with a shot into the rough in front of the green. But Woods then hit a beautiful, high wedge shot that stopped 15 feet from the hole, giving him a chance for a tying birdie on the par-5 hole.

The putt curled slightly to the left. Then it dropped into the cup, giving Woods a tie for the lead and setting up an 18-hole playoff with Mediate the next day.

"MARKO" AND THE TIGER

Woods kept his circle of friends on the PGA Tour small. He liked privacy. Mark O'Meara, a longtime PGA Tour player almost 20 years older than Woods, became his closest friend on tour. It was an unlikely pairing, but both were from Southern California and quickly became friends. When Woods moved to Orlando, Florida, after turning pro, he and the O'Meara family, who lived nearby, spent a lot of time together. One night Alicia O'Meara told her husband, "That poor kid is sitting over there in his house all alone. Let's get him over for dinner." Woods, who calls his friend "Marko," said he became like his big brother.[9]

Woods rejoices after sinking a birdie putt to close out the fourth round and force a playoff with Rocco Mediate at the 2008 US Open.

"I don't think there was a person on the planet who was watching who didn't think he was going to make it," said golfer Tom Lehman. "I was thinking that Rocco should be getting his beauty rest because he'll be in a playoff."[10]

Fittingly, the one-on-one duel was dramatic. Woods and Mediate went back and forth all day, taking turns in the lead. Again, Woods was forced to make a birdie putt on 18 to tie again and send the match to an extra hole. On that nineteenth hole, Mediate made bogey and Woods made a par to give him the US Open title.

Woods, with his fourteenth major championship, said he thought his victory was "probably the best ever," considering his injuries and the drama over five days and ninety-one holes.[11] Haney, who knew how much pain Woods endured, was amazed.

"I've never come close to seeing anything like that show," Haney said. "Going in, I didn't know what was going to happen. Three weeks before the US Open, he couldn't walk."[12]

"With his 14 career majors, Woods has crept ever closer to Nicklaus's epic total of 18, and it is mind-boggling to think that at 32 he is potentially one great calendar year away from attaining the unattainable."[13]

— **Sports Illustrated** *story after Woods's US Open victory in 2008*

THE FALL

The victory at the 2008 US Open came with a cost. Two days after winning, Woods announced he had a double stress fracture in his left leg and also needed reconstructive knee surgery for torn ligaments. His year was over. He would need months to heal and rehabilitate his injuries.

Woods didn't make his official return until March 2009, an absence of nine months. At the Arnold Palmer Invitational in Florida, he showed he hadn't forgotten how to win. He charged back from a five-shot deficit at the start of the fourth round to get the victory with a birdie on the final hole.

Woods was back on the winning track two weeks before the first major of the season, the Masters. Yet he fell short at the Masters. In fact, he went winless in the first three majors of 2009, finishing in a tie for sixth at the Masters and the US Open and missing the cut at the British Open.

Tiger Woods's world came crashing down around him in 2009.

At the PGA Championship, however, Woods opened with a brilliant 5-under-par 67, followed by a 70 and a 71 in the next two rounds to go into Sunday with a two-stroke lead.

SHOCKING COLLAPSE

Woods was a virtual lock to earn his fifteenth major. As he stood on the first tee that day at Hazeltine National Golf Club in Minnesota, he was 14–0 in major tournaments when holding at least a share of the lead through three rounds. This time, however, would be different.

Woods bogeyed two holes on the front nine and three on the back while shooting a 3-over-par 75. Y. E. Yang of South Korea, who entered the day two shots behind Woods, had an eagle and two birdies in a round of 70 to win.

It was a stunning loss for Woods, considering Yang had just one previous victory on the PGA Tour. But all day, it was Yang who made the clutch shots, not Woods.

For the first time since 2004, Woods had not won a major tournament. As it turned out, his troubles were just beginning.

Since turning professional in 1996, Woods, his management team, and his sponsors had created a favorable public image of the golfer. To the public, Woods

A dejected Woods walks off the course after his shocking loss to Y. E. Yang at the 2009 PGA Championship.

was a wholesome, hardworking, talented athlete and a devoted family man. By late 2009, Tiger and his wife, Elin, appeared to be a model couple. Their second child, son Charlie, was born in February. At 33, Woods and his family lived in a $2.4 million mansion near Orlando, Florida, and he was reported to be the first US athlete to earn

NO LONGER UNBEATABLE

When Woods lost the 2009 PGA Championship to Y. E. Yang, some PGA Tour players weren't sad. Woods up to that point in his career had seemed invincible. An attendant in the player's clubhouse told a reporter that players were watching the Yang-Woods duel with interest. "You have no idea how many players were down there cheering Yang on, jumping up and down on the couch just to see Tiger finally get beat," he said.[2]

$1 billion. Sponsors lined up to sign deals with him, and he earned about $110 million per year in endorsements.[1]

Woods's image was carefully guarded. Few reporters were allowed one-on-one access to him, and at news conferences he rarely offered much other than bland comments about golf. In fact, after a lengthy profile in GQ magazine in 1997 that revealed Woods as a 21-year-old who sometimes swore, told racy jokes, and flirted with women, Woods only let his guard down around his inner circle. Those family and friends came to be known as Team Tiger.

FALL FROM GRACE

But in late November 2009, the National Enquirer tabloid published a cover story featuring an ominous headline: "Tiger Woods Cheating Scandal." The story reported Woods had been having an affair for many months with a woman from New York City. The story said the woman

DECEMBER 14, 2009

WEEKLY

Issue 774
December 14, 2009

H
Bab
Lou
Sulola
Samuel

People

ONLY IN Us

'Lin
Ne
Caug
Alba

YES, HE
CHEATED

TIGER IN
ROUBLE

Hotel hookups,
dirty texts —
Tiger's mistress of
3 years tells all.
PLUS His panic after
Elin found out

"He said,
'We will
always be
together'"

JAKE
Is
Tro

SIDE THE SCANDAL A late-night car
h and rumors of infidelity: Is the squea
n golfer's marriage on the rocks?

Tiger and Elin couldn't escape the spotlight as news of his infidelity spread.

had traveled to be with Woods earlier in November at the Australian Masters golf tournament, which Woods won.

Woods assured his wife the story was wrong, but she was skeptical. The next day, on Thanksgiving night, after her husband had gone to bed, Elin got on Tiger's cell phone and called the woman, telling her, "I know everything."[3] Soon Tiger was awakened by his wife's angry screams. She threw the cell phone at him. It hit him in the

Woods took full responsibility for his actions in a statement at a press briefing on February 19, 2010.

face and chipped one of his teeth. Eventually she grabbed a golf club and chased him from the house at 2:30 a.m.

When Tiger hurriedly tried to leave, Elin smashed two back windows of his vehicle. He crashed the vehicle into a fire hydrant and a tree. When neighbors called the police about the disturbance, officers found Woods on the ground, with cuts on his face. An ambulance took him to a hospital.

In the days after the incident, Woods issued a statement saying the incident was a "private matter" and that he was responsible for his accident.[4]

Over the next weeks, several other women claimed to have had affairs with Woods. In fact, for many years he had been spending time with women other than Elin, especially after the death of his father in 2006. Tiger often had disagreements with Earl because his father had affairs, which caused a rift that prompted Earl and Kultida to live in separate houses. But out of the public eye, Woods had been following his father's example.

TAKING RESPONSIBILITY

In late December 2009, Woods started therapy. Then, on February 19, Woods held a news conference that was televised nationally. He read a statement saying he'd been irresponsible and selfish and that he had spent 45 days in counseling.

"I know I have bitterly disappointed all of you," he said.

EMBRACING BUDDHISM

After apologizing for his affairs in 2010, Woods said he had strayed from his Buddhist faith, which he'd learned from his mother. He said he intended to embrace those beliefs again to get back on track. "Buddhism teaches that a craving of things outside ourselves causes an unhappy and pointless search for security," he said. "It teaches me to stop following every impulse and to learn restraint."[5]

"For all that I have done, I am so sorry. . . . I had affairs. I cheated. What I did was not acceptable, and I am the only person to blame."[6]

Many of Woods's sponsors quickly cut their association with him, and he stayed away from the game until April, when he entered the Masters. After playing his first practice round at Augusta, he held a news conference and again apologized for his actions. He said his perceptions and priorities had now changed.

"It's not about the championships," he said. "It's about how you live your life."[7]

Woods finished tied for fourth, a surprisingly good showing after a long layoff. But the rest of the year, his game was far from what it had been. He didn't win a single tournament. And his year was filled with change. His swing coach, Hank Haney, left, citing a "dysfunctional" relationship.[8] And in August he turned in one

PAY CUT

After news of Woods's extramarital affairs became public in 2009, many companies decided to drop him from endorsement deals. Accenture, AT&T, Gatorade, and Gillette were among those to cut ties with their onetime star client. By one estimate, Woods lost $22 million in endorsements in 2010.[9] However, Nike—Woods's first major sponsor—decided to stand by him. Phil Knight, the company's chair, said he was confident Woods would work his way through his problems. "When his career is over, you'll look back on these indiscretions as a minor blip," he said.[10] A spokesperson for Gatorade, however, said, "We no longer see a role for Tiger in our marketing efforts and have ended our relationship."[11]

of the poorest performances of his career, shooting over par all four rounds at the Bridgestone Invitational in Ohio. Approximately three weeks later, Tiger and Elin Woods announced their divorce.

After 281 consecutive weeks ranked number one in the world, Woods dropped to second on November 1, 2010. The last time he had lost the top ranking, in 2004, he regained it in 27 weeks. This time, after a winless year and personal problems, some doubted he'd ever get back to the top.

"His golf peers are not afraid of him anymore, and there seems to be a new crop of players coming up and the Tiger era is already finished," said Peter Thomson, a retired, five-time British Open champion.[12]

"I honestly didn't know what to expect from the fans, but they were absolutely incredible. It was unreal. They definitely helped me mentally be more comfortable out there. To get that type of warmth is something I did not expect and will never forget."[13]

— *Tiger Woods on his return to golf in April 2010 after his public marital scandal*

TRYING TO
BOUNCE BACK

I t was a bright, beautiful Florida afternoon, and Woods was smiling again, just like old times. Woods, wearing his trademark Sunday red shirt, tapped in a short putt for par on last hole, threw a victory punch with his right fist, and shouted "Yeah!"[1] He had just won the Arnold Palmer Invitational in Orlando on March 25, 2012, by five shots.

Woods, now 36, hugged his caddie, Joe LaCava, and waved his hat to the gallery to acknowledge their applause. He was beaming.

"It's not like winning a major championship or anything," he said later. "But it certainly feels really good."[2]

It was Woods's first victory in a PGA Tour event in 923 days, dating to September 2009, two months before his world was turned upside down after the revelation of his lies and

Tiger Woods was determined to return to form after a tumultuous period in his career and personal life.

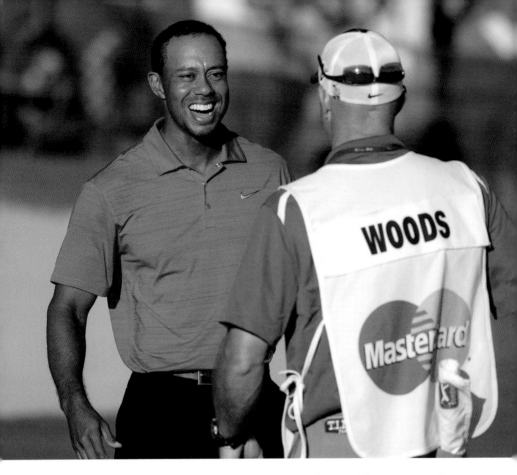

Woods and caddie Joe LaCava celebrate after Woods's victory at the Arnold Palmer Invitational in March 2012.

marital infidelities. The man who used to win tournaments in bunches had gone 26 consecutive official events without a win. Woods went 0-for-2010 and 0-for-2011 before finally winning his fifth start of 2012.

And, the win came just two weeks after having to withdraw from an event because of pain in his left Achilles tendon. An injury in the same spot at the 2011 Masters forced him to miss almost four months and two majors. This time, the pain subsided and Woods was able to come back quickly to play the Palmer event.

The victory lifted him to sixth in the world rankings. He hadn't been in the top ten since May 2011. "I am excited, no doubt," Woods said. "I'm looking forward to the momentum I've built here."[3]

NOT SO FAST

But Woods and the fans still pulling for him would ride a roller coaster the next five seasons, with a few scattered ups overshadowed by many downs. He no longer was the physically fit young star who seemed immune to pressure. Injuries to his knee, Achilles tendon, and back put him on the sidelines for weeks or months at a time.

In 2012, Woods had two more wins and was in contention at the British Open but finished in a tie for third. He built on that in 2013, winning five times. After winning the Arnold Palmer Invitational again in March, he regained the top ranking in the world for the first time in three years and was voted the tour's Player of the Year.

CADDIE AND BUDDY

Joe LaCava started as Woods's caddie in 2011. LaCava replaced Steve Williams, who was with Woods for 12 years. LaCava refused to work for any other golfer during Woods's string of injuries and disappointments. Woods said LaCava's loyalty during that time was appreciated. "He's positive, upbeat, competitive," said Woods in 2018. "Man, he's into it and he's been a great friend over the years, but especially the last couple of years when it's been tough."[4]

Woods struggled to find consistency as he battled numerous injuries.

Still, the closest he could come to a major title was a tie for fourth at the Masters.

After two solid seasons, Woods hoped to finally win his fifteenth major title in 2014. But just before the Masters that April, Woods, now 38, had to have back surgery. He'd been playing with pain but could no longer cope. He missed three months and didn't win a single tournament in 2014.

PAIN CONTINUES

In 2015, Woods again was in pain and had to have surgery in September after missing the cut in three of the four majors. That was followed by another surgery on his back a month later to relieve discomfort. Woods had to sit out all of 2016. When he tried coming back in 2017, he missed the cut in his only official event. A few weeks later he had to have his fourth back surgery, this time to fuse discs in his lower back.

"I could no longer live with the pain I had," said Woods. "We tried every possible non-surgical route and nothing worked." His back was painful even when lying down. After surgery, however, he felt "instant relief."[5]

A month later, Woods was found asleep in his car alongside a road in Florida and arrested and charged with driving under the influence. He blamed the incident

OLYMPIC MATCHUP

When Woods and Olympic alpine skier Lindsey Vonn began a relationship in 2012, they became a focus of media attention. The three-time Olympic medalist and 14-time majors winner were subjects of magazine stories and photographers until they split in 2015. Woods then moved into a long relationship with Erica Herman. She accompanied him to many of his tournaments.

Meanwhile, Woods and his ex-wife Elin became good friends again. They often talked as they raised their son and daughter. "She's one of my best friends," Woods said. "We're able to pick up the phone and we talk to each other all the time. We both know that the most important things in our lives are our kids. I wish I would have known that back then."[6]

on not properly managing his pain medications and entered a program to learn how to better handle his prescribed medicines.

As 2018 approached, Woods said he felt better than he had in years. He was free of pain and able to practice again to sharpen his skills. In December, he played well in a non-PGA Tour event in the Bahamas and was excited by his health and his game. As he approached his forty-second birthday, he was driving the ball as far as he ever had and putting well, too. He was excited by his "bright future."[7]

But would he be able to maintain that quality and his fitness over the grind of a long season? After all, both he and the tour had changed since he won his last major in 2008. Woods had lost some of the magic he held over opponents. Four-time major champion Ernie Els, who had once been the world's top player, said it was almost impossible to beat Woods in his prime because Woods never believed he

FASTEST SWING ON TOUR AGAIN

In 2008 when Woods won the US Open, his swing speed was 125 miles per hour (201 kmh). By 2014, it had fallen to 116 mph (187 kmh).[8] When Woods finally regained his health in 2018, it was all the way up to 129 mph (208 kmh), the fastest on the PGA Tour that season.[9] With a healthy back, his swing was strong and smooth again. "Now I don't feel like I'm swinging very hard, but it's producing some incredible speeds," he said.[10]

Young players such as Rory McIlroy, right, looked up to Woods but weren't intimidated by him.

would lose. "I believe that no one is going to break his hold on the game until that mindset is broken," said Els.[11]

COMPETITION SURGES

By 2012, that mind-set was shattered, and other golfers knew Woods was beatable. A new crop of young stars in their early 20s—Rory McIlroy, Rickie Fowler, Keegan Bradley, Jason Day, and Brandt Snedeker—was coming on fast. Jordan Spieth, Justin Thomas and Brooks Koepka would soon follow.

In many ways, all of them were similar to Woods in that they valued fitness and strength and could hit the ball a long way. But none had played against the Woods who won 14 major titles over 12 years. They admired him for what he'd done, but they didn't fear him. They'd watched him on TV as kids, and now he was from a previous generation.

As Woods struggled, the young stars thrived. In 2011, Bradley won the PGA Championship and McIlroy took the US Open. McIlroy added the PGA in 2012 and the British Open in 2014. By 2017, Spieth had won the Masters, US Open, and British Open.

So, when Woods began his 2018 comeback, it was a new landscape. After falling out of the top 1,000 in the world rankings in 2017, would Woods be able to compete with golf's new breed?

The answer was yes. Woods played 18 tour events in 2018, his most since 2012, and he finished the year healthy. He briefly held the lead in the final round of the British Open before finishing three strokes

COACHING CAROUSEL

As Woods struggled with inconsistency both on the course and with his health, he began working with his third pro swing coach, Sean Foley, in 2010. But Woods never found much success with Foley. In 56 events with Foley, Woods won just eight times, with no majors. By the time Woods made his healthy comeback in 2018, he'd decided to go without a coach and manage his own swing through video analysis.

behind the leader. Then, in the final round of the PGA Championship, he shot a terrific 6-under-par 64 on the Bellerive Country Club course in Saint Louis, Missouri, to finish second by two shots to Koepka. It was Woods's lowest final-round score ever in a major tournament. As the day unfolded, the gallery following him around the course grew larger and louder, just the way it was in his heyday. Fans yelled encouragement and climbed trees to get a better view. Course marshals had to keep some young fans from running onto the fairways.

COMEBACK . . . KID?

Yet Woods saved his best for last. At the annual Tour Championship, the final event of the season, Woods shot 65-68-65 over the first three rounds to get to 12 under par on the East Lake course in Atlanta, giving him a three-shot lead. In the final round, he birdied the first hole to increase his lead to four strokes. He was solid the rest of the day and won by two shots. Throughout the tournament, he was cheered by a loud gallery, which grew larger on the final day. At the victory ceremony, the usually stoic Woods was emotional, talking about his first victory on tour in five years. "I was having a hard time not crying coming up the last hole," he said.[12]

"I've exceeded all of my expectations and goals because so much was unknown. When I was laying on the ground and couldn't move for a number of months, golf was the furthest thing from my mind. To have gone through that and got to this point, it's good fun."[15]

— Tiger Woods, on rebounding from back pain and surgery to have a strong 2018 season.

Finally, he believed he was back, and he loved being competitive again after being away for so long. At many times in the past few years, he didn't know if he'd ever win again.

"I loved every bit of it," he said. "The fight and the grind and the tough conditions, and just had to suck it up and hit shots, and I loved every bit of it."[13]

Watching Woods on TV was his boyhood idol, Jack Nicklaus. After Woods sunk his winning putt, Nicklaus tweeted his congratulations and praised him. "I never dreamed Tiger Woods could come back and swing the way he has after surgery," wrote Nicklaus. "I think you could argue he's swinging better than he ever has in his life. He has played fantastically!"[14]

As he approached age 43, Woods had his eightieth PGA Tour win, two behind Sam Snead's record. He rebounded all the way back to number 13 in the world

Woods emerges from a sea of fans at Atlanta's East Lake Golf Club as he walks up the fairway on the final hole of his victory at the 2018 Tour Championship.

rankings at the end of 2018 and to sixth after his Masters victory in 2019. But mainly, he was just happy to be playing at a high level again.

"I've still got a chance to play some more golf, and maybe I'll keep chipping away at that number and maybe surpass it," Woods said. "But I just think that what I've gone through and what I've dealt with, I've gotten lucky, to be honest with you. I've gotten very lucky."[16]

LEGACY

When Woods won the Masters in 1997, many predicted he would change golf forever. They believed the sight of an athletic, talented, 21-year-old mixed-race man conquering Augusta National Golf Club and beating the best players would lead young children of color to take up the game.

Lee Elder, who broke the color barrier at the Masters in 1975, compared Woods to Jackie Robinson, the Hall of Fame baseball player. Robinson opened the door to a tidal wave of talented black players when he broke his sport's color barrier in 1947. Elder called Woods's victory at Augusta "one happy and glorious day."[1]

"All blacks have hoped and prayed for a day like this to come," said Elder on the day of Woods's victory. "I felt like it would, but I didn't think it'd be this soon with this young man."[2]

But the promised increase of black golfers was never fulfilled. More than 20 years after Woods's

Tiger Woods has cast a long shadow in the golf world.

Lee Elder, left, embraces Woods after Woods's historic victory at the 1997 Masters.

breakthrough victory, he remains the only prominent American player of color on the PGA Tour. Through 2018, Harold Varner III and Joseph Bramlett were the only black players to earn a PGA Tour card since Woods.

FANS, NOT PLAYERS

Edward Wanambwa, the senior editor of *African American Golfer's Digest*, recalls watching Woods at the 1997 Masters with some of his family, most of whom didn't care about golf. But that weekend, they turned on the Masters to watch a black man win in a traditionally white sport. "There was this expectation that it was going to open the floodgates for more African-American players in the game," Wanambwa said. "But that never materialized."[3]

During Woods's peak years, more black fans came out to tournaments or watched him on TV. They were part of a wave of greater interest in the game caused by Woods. The United States had 24 million golfers in 1996, a total that grew to 31 million by 2003. But by 2015, when Woods had all but vanished from the tour because of injuries, that number was back to 24 million.[4] Black players were a small part of that boom. The National Golf Foundation reported that in 1999, two years after Woods made headlines at the Masters, there were more than 880,000 black golfers in the United States, up 145 percent from 1986.[5]

But the black participation didn't keep growing at that rate. By 2010, the 1.4 million black golfers made up just 5 percent of the total in the United States.[6] And there was no surge of black youth through junior programs, high schools, and colleges into the PGA Tour or its lower pro ranks. In fact, in 2018 even historically black colleges and universities in the United States had trouble filling their rosters with black golfers.

The reasons are many, but the biggest is that golf is expensive due to the equipment, coaching, and travel demands. Plus, the best competition is still found at country clubs, says Wendell Haskins, former head of diversity for the Professional Golfers Association of America. "You have to have access to elite golf to play elite golf," said Haskins.[7]

Woods says the rising use of golf carts has killed caddie programs at public and private courses. That change has closed doors for African Americans who want to learn the game and play it. Elder learned the game as a caddie, and so did other black players before Woods such as Jim Dent and Charlie Sifford.

LASTING LEGACY

Despite the fact Woods's brilliance didn't inspire greater numbers of black golfers to the PGA Tour, Woods's legacy as one of the greatest and most influential players in the sport's history is secure. And his influence extends beyond

Woods was joined at the White House by, from left, girlfriend Erica Herman, mother Kultida, daughter Sam Alexis, and son Charlie when he received the Presidential Medal of Freedom.

the golf course. On May 6, 2019, Woods was invited to the White House, where President Donald Trump honored him with the Presidential Medal of Freedom. The award is the highest honor a US president can give a civilian.

Woods left his mark on his fellow golfers, too. Before Woods joined the tour, people often debated whether golfers were even athletes. Since Woods arrived, there's been no question. He looked and worked out like an athlete, and the players who've followed him into golf's elite level have done the same.

And his length off the tee inspired a younger generation to swing and attack the ball just as he did. When he came on tour in 1996, few players hit the ball 300 yards off the tee. By 2018, Woods was still averaging 303.6 yards at age 42, but he ranked tied for thirty-second behind leader Rory McIlroy's 319.7. Like Woods, McIlroy is a dedicated fitness fanatic who lifts weights, stretches, and works on strength and flexibility.

Just as Jack Nicklaus inspired Woods as a boy, Woods inspired McIlroy when McIlroy was growing up in Northern Ireland. McIlroy remembers watching Woods's win at Augusta in 1997 and had his poster on his wall. "He was the inspiration for us to go out and try to be the best that we could be," said McIlroy. "He was a hero to us growing up, and that's why you have so many guys in their early twenties that are so good right now."[8]

Woods's arrival as a pro boosted TV ratings, attendance, sponsors, and prize money. When he was on the course, whether at age 21 or 42, he drew huge galleries. He made golf cool to watch and play. Chris Riley, a PGA Tour pro, Ryder Cup teammate and youth rival of Woods, said the sport was "nerdy" before Woods, but Tiger "transcended the game" to take it mainstream.[9]

"Where do I see myself in the next five to ten years? I'm still playing golf at the highest level and winning tournaments and major championships."[10]

— *Tiger Woods in 2018*

How dominant was Woods in his prime? From 1999 through 2003, he won 32 times on the PGA Tour. No other player won more than eight times. And, over the time between his first major title in 1997 and his fourteenth in 2008, he was a combined 126 under par in majors, 189 shots better than anyone else who had played at least 40 rounds in that span.

He was perhaps even greater on the greens than he was off the tee, too. How good? From 2002 through 2005 he had 1,540 putts from three feet or closer in tour events and only missed three.

INTANGIBLES

But those are just the numbers. There was also the Tiger swagger and how he intimidated his opponents. His focused demeanor while playing, the sound of his driver when it made contact with the ball, and his deadly

Woods rejoices after completing his comeback at the 2019 Masters.

accurate putting in major championships were just too much for some opponents to handle. Hall of Fame golfer Tom Weiskopf, who played against champions such as Nicklaus and Ben Hogan, compared Woods to Superman. "The way he was marketed, the answers he gave, the aura of invincibility," said Weiskopf. "There was practically an 'S' on his chest."[11]

Earl Woods said his son was extremely competitive as a boy. He wanted to win at everything. Woods, even after his fortieth birthday, acknowledged that is what drove him. He loved to be challenged and come out on top. "Winning was fun," said Woods. "Beating someone's even better."[12]

Golf has had many great players, including Nicklaus, Arnold Palmer, Sam Snead, Hogan, Bobby Jones, and Gary Player. But to McIlroy and many of those who followed Woods, Tiger is supreme.

"That 10-year stretch of golf is the best stretch of golf we have ever seen on the planet by anyone," said McIlroy. "I don't care what anyone says about Jack Nicklaus's record or anyone else. That 10-year stretch of golf was the best. And I don't know if anyone's going to emulate that at all, but I think people need to remember that. Because he has been and is the greatest player that has ever played this game."[13]

"Golf is better when Tiger is around. I don't know if we need Tiger. We all want Tiger. I want to see Tiger playing again. It's fun. He has an innate ability to do things that only a couple of guys in the world can do."[15]
— PGA Tour player Brandt Snedeker

TIMELINE

1975
On December 30, Tiger Woods is born in Cypress, California.

1978
Tiger appears on *The Mike Douglas Show* on October 6, demonstrating his putting and driving skills to the delight of Douglas and his guests, comedian Bob Hope and actor Jimmy Stewart.

1994
Tiger becomes the youngest player ever to win the US Amateur championship. It is the first of his three straight US Amateur titles; in September, Woods enrolls at Stanford University.

1996
Woods wins his first PGA Tour event, the Las Vegas Invitational.

1997
Woods wins the Masters at Augusta National, his first major championship in golf. At 21, he's the youngest Masters winner.

2001
Woods wins the Masters to become the first player to hold all four major titles at the same time. The feat becomes known as the "Tiger Slam."

2004
On October 5, Woods and Elin Nordegren are married in Barbados.

2006

Earl Woods, Tiger's father and closest friend, dies.

2007

In June, Woods becomes a father for the first time with the birth of his daughter, Sam.

2008

Woods beats Rocco Mediate in a 19-hole playoff to win the US Open, his fourteenth major championship.

2010

Tiger and Elin file for divorce.

2013

Woods is named PGA Tour Player of the Year for the eleventh time, but the first since 2009.

2016-2017

Woods undergoes multiple back surgeries.

2018

Woods wins the PGA Tour Championship, his first win on tour since 2013 and his eightieth PGA Tour win overall.

2019

On April 14, Woods wins his fifteenth major with a one-shot victory at the Masters; on May 6, President Donald Trump awards Woods the Presidential Medal of Freedom, the highest honor a US president can bestow on a civilian.

ESSENTIAL FACTS

FULL NAME
Eldrick Tont Woods. Nickname: Tiger

DATE OF BIRTH
December 30, 1975

PLACE OF BIRTH
Cypress, California

PARENTS
Earl and Kultida Woods

MARRIAGE
Elin Nordegren (2004–2010)

CHILDREN
Sam Alexis and Charlie

EDUCATION
Attended Stanford University for two years

CAREER HIGHLIGHTS
- The 2019 Masters victory was Woods's fifteenth major golf championship, second only to Jack Nicklaus's 18.

- In 1997, Woods became the youngest player to win the Masters.

- His 81 victories on the PGA Tour through the 2019 Masters left him two behind Sam Snead for the all-time record.

- In 2001, he completed the "Tiger Slam" by winning the Masters, giving him all four major titles at the same time.

- As of 2018, he was the only player to win the US Amateur championship three times.

- Between 1998 and 2005, Woods made the cut in 142 consecutive events. The previous record had been 113.

- In 2000, his scoring average per round was 68.17, breaking the mark of 68.33 set in 1945.

- Through 2018 he'd been ranked number one in the world a total of 683 weeks. Greg Norman is second, with 331 weeks at number one.

- Woods won 46 events in his twenties, 16 more than Nicklaus.

- He led the money list in ten seasons and had more than $115 million in winnings through 2018.

- He won the Vardon Trophy for lowest scoring average nine times, four more than any other player.

- In 2019, President Donald Trump awarded Woods the Presidential Medal of Freedom, the highest honor a US president can bestow on a civilian.

CONFLICTS

Woods admitted to a series of affairs that led to the end of his marriage to Elin Nordegren and tarnished his previously wholesome image. The scandal, which cost him millions in potential sponsorship revenue, coincided with a steep decline in his success on the course.

QUOTE

"The bigger the event, the higher he'll raise the bar. He's Michael Jordan in long pants."

—Golfer Paul Azinger after watching Woods's first Masters victory

GLOSSARY

amateur

A person who competes in a sport without payment.

birdie

A score one stroke below the designated par for a hole, such as shooting a four on a par-5 hole.

bogey

A score one stroke above the designated par for a hole, such as shooting a five on a par-4 hole. A double bogey is two strokes above par.

bunker

Also known as a sand trap, a bunker is an obstacle filled with sand alongside a fairway or green.

caddie

A person who accompanies a pro golfer on the course, carries the clubs, and provides advice about which club to use for a particular shot.

cut

The process of eliminating players with the highest scores midway through a tournament. Players who miss the cut are not allowed to play the final two rounds.

driver

A golfer's longest club, with the least loft on its clubface, used to hit the ball off a tee on longer holes.

eagle

A score two strokes below the designated par for a hole, such as shooting a three on a par-5 hole.

fairway

The route from tee to green on every hole, on which the grass is kept short. The fairway is the ideal landing spot for the golfer's tee shot, providing the best conditions for the next shot.

gallery

The crowd watching a golfer during a tournament.

green

The area around the hole, where the grass is cut its shortest. Once on the green, golfers use a putter to knock the ball into the hole.

majors

The four designated biggest events in golf each year: the Masters, PGA Championship, US Open, and British Open.

par

The number of strokes expected for a particular hole, usually determined by the hole's length and difficulty. A par-3 hole is the shortest, while par-4 and par-5 holes are longer. Courses also have a total par, which is the sum of all 18 holes. Most commonly, it is 72.

PGA Tour

The series of professional tournaments held each year across the United States. Golfers must qualify to play on the tour.

rough

The tall, thick grass that grows alongside fairways.

tee

Also known as the tee box or teeing ground, it is the spot at the start of a hole where golfers hit their first shot. Tee also refers to the small wooden or plastic item that is placed into the ground to support the golf ball when it is hit at the tee box.

wedge

A very short club with a lot of loft on its clubface. It is used to lob or chip a shot from a short distance onto the green.

ADDITIONAL RESOURCES

SELECTED BIBLIOGRAPHY

Callahan, Tom. *His Father's Son: Earl and Tiger Woods*. New York: Gotham Books, 2010.

O'Connor, Ian. "After Yang Took Down Tiger, Major Golf Was Never the Same." *ESPN*. 11 Aug. 2015. ESPN.com.

FURTHER READINGS

Glave, Tom. *Tiger Woods vs. Jack Nicklaus*. Minneapolis, MN: Abdo, 2018.

Sowell, David. *The Masters: A Hole-by-Hole History of America's Golf Classic*. Lincoln, NE: University of Nebraska Press, 2019.

Woods, Tiger. *The 1997 Masters: My Story*. New York: Hachette, 2017.

ONLINE RESOURCES

Booklinks
NONFICTION NETWORK
FREE! ONLINE NONFICTION RESOURCES

To learn more about Tiger Woods, please visit **abdobooklinks.com** or scan this QR code. These links are routinely monitored and updated to provide the most current information available.

MORE INFORMATION

For more information on this subject, contact or visit the following organizations:

PGA OF AMERICA
100 Avenue of the Champions
Palm Beach Gardens, FL 33418
561-624-8400
pga.com/home

The PGA of America is one of the world's largest sports organizations, with nearly 29,000 PGA professionals who work daily to grow interest and participation in the game of golf.

UNITED STATES GOLF ASSOCIATION MUSEUM
77 Liberty Corner Road
Liberty Corner, NJ 07938
908-234-2300
usgamuseum.com

Opened in 1951 in New York City, this museum was moved to New Jersey in 1972. It houses a large collection of memorabilia from top American golfers and national championships governed by the US Golf Association.

WORLD GOLF HALL OF FAME
1 World Golf Place
Saint Augustine, FL 32092
904-940-4000
worldgolfhalloffame.org

This museum honors the contributions and accomplishments of golfers from across the globe. It originally was opened in Pinehurst, North Carolina, in 1974. It moved to Florida in 1998.

SOURCE NOTES

CHAPTER 1. MASTERFUL

1. "Tiger (67): Gotta 'Get the Mind and Body Ready for Tomorrow.'" *Golf Channel*, 13 Apr. 2019, golfchannel.com. Accessed 6 May 2019.

2. Brian Pascus. "Tiger Woods Wins 2019 Masters to Capture First Green Jacket Since 2005." *CBS News*, 14 Apr. 2019, cbsnews.com. Accessed 6 May 2019.

CHAPTER 2. YOUNG TIGER

1. Thomas Neumann. "Tiger Woods: 40 for 40." *ESPN*, 29 Dec. 2015, espn.com. Accessed 27 Feb. 2019.

2. Bill Fields. "The Genius of Earl Woods." *Golf Digest*, 8 July 2008, golfdigest.com. Accessed 27 Feb. 2019.

3. Fields, "The Genius of Earl Woods."

4. Fields, "The Genius of Earl Woods."

5. John Strege. "Has the Genius Been Coached Out of Tiger Woods? His First Instructor Says No." *Golf Digest*, 30 June 2015, golfdigest.com. Accessed 27 Feb. 2019.

6. Tod Leonard. "Junior World Golf: 50th Playing Stirs Indelible Memories." *San Diego Union-Tribune*, 7 July 2017, sandiegouniontribune.com. Accessed 27 Feb. 2019.

7. Steve DiMeglio. "Tiger Woods Opens Up about His Parents' Influence on His Career." *USA Today*, 3 Apr. 2017, usatoday.com. Accessed 27 Feb. 2019.

8. Ryan Lavner. "Reliving Tiger's PGA Tour Debut at Riviera." *Golf Channel*, 13 Feb. 2017, golfchannel.com. Accessed 27 Feb. 2019.

9. Alex Myers. "Look, Tiger Woods Really Did Have a Jack Nicklaus Poster in His Childhood Bedroom." *Golf Digest*, 15 Oct. 2015, golfdigest.com. Accessed 27 Feb. 2019.

10. Neumann, "Tiger Woods: 40 for 40."

11. Lavner, "Reliving Tiger's PGA Tour Debut at Riviera."

12. "Tiger Woods' 40 Biggest Moments: Winning a Third Straight U.S. Junior Amateur Title." *Golf*, 27 Nov. 2015, golf.com. Accessed 27 Feb. 2019.

13. Tom Callahan. *His Father's Son: Earl and Tiger Woods*. Penguin, 2010.

CHAPTER 3. "HELLO, WORLD"

1. Martin Beck. "High School Signings: Woods Says Stanford Suits His Game—and Lifestyle." *Los Angeles Times*, 11 Nov. 1993, articles.latimes.com. Accessed 28 Feb. 2019.

2. Jeff Bradley. "First Class Tiger." *ESPN*, 29 Mar. 2013, en.espn.co.uk. Accessed 28 Feb. 2019.

3. "Recalling Tiger's First Masters Visit, 20 Years Ago Today: 'Magnolia Lane, Is That It?'" *Golf Digest*, n.d., golfdigest.com. Accessed 28 Feb. 2019.

4. Jaime Diaz. "Roaring Ahead: The Story of Tiger Woods' 1996 US Amateur Win." *Golf*, 16 Aug. 2012, golf.com. Accessed 28 Feb. 2019.

5. Joe Passov. "Tiger's 40 Biggest Moments: No. 16—'Hello World' Advertisement." *Golf*, 15 Dec. 2015, golf.com. Accessed 28 Feb. 2019.

6. Bob Harig. "Tiger Woods Signs New Nike Deal." *ESPN*, 17 July 2013, espn.com. Accessed 1 Mar. 2019.

7. "Tiger Woods Sponsorship Deals and Endorsements." *Telegraph*, 1 Dec. 2009, telegraph.co.uk. Accessed 1 Mar. 2019.

8. Passov, "Tiger's 40 Biggest Moments."

9. Passov, "Tiger's 40 Biggest Moments."

10. Steve Bornfeld. "Tiger's Roar: Woods Claims First PGA Tour Win in Las Vegas, Oct. 6, 1996." *Las Vegas Newswire*, 2 Oct. 2018, lasvegasnewswire.com. Accessed 28 Feb. 2019.

11. Bornfeld, "Tiger's Roar."

12. Rick Reilly. "Top Cat a Two-Time Winner in Only a Few Weeks, Tiger Woods Has Become the Man to Beat." *Sports Illustrated Vault*, 28 Oct. 1996, si.com. Accessed 28 Feb. 2019.

CHAPTER 4. SUPERSTAR

1. Scott Michaux. "Woods' Runaway Victory in 1997 Masters Shook Sport." *Augusta Chronicle*, 31 Mar. 2017, augusta.com. Accessed 27 Feb. 2019.

2. Michaux, "Woods' Runaway Victory in 1997 Masters Shook Sport."

3. Adam Stanley. "20 Awesome Facts about Tiger Woods' Epic 1997 Masters Win." *SN*, 2 Apr. 2017, sportsnet.ca. Accessed 27 Feb. 2019.

4. "Tiger Woods: Looking Back at 1997." *Augusta Chronicle*, 10 Feb. 2017, augusta.com. Accessed 27 Feb. 2019.

5. Ryan Lavner. "The 1997 Masters, and the Impact 20 Years Later." *Golf Channel*, 28 Mar. 2017, golfchannel.com. Accessed 27 Feb. 2019.

6. Michaux, "Woods' Runaway Victory in 1997 Masters Shook Sport."

7. Michaux, "Woods' Runaway Victory in 1997 Masters Shook Sport."

8. Rick Reilly. "Tiger Woods Wins the 1997 Masters by 12 Shots." *Golf*, 10 Nov. 2011, golf.com. Accessed 27 Feb. 2019.

CHAPTER 5. CHARGING AHEAD

1. Ed Sherman. "Tiger's Time?" *Chicago Tribune*, 24 June 1998, chicagotribune.com. Accessed 28 Feb. 2019.

2. Thomas Neumann. "Tiger Woods: 40 for 40." *ESPN*, 29 Dec. 2015, espn.com. Accessed 28 Feb. 2019.

3. John Garrity. "Tiger Woods Wins the 2000 US Open at Pebble Beach by 15 Strokes." *Golf*, 19 Aug. 2011, golf.com. Accessed 28 Feb. 2019.

4. "Woods Grabs Piece of History at Augusta." *ESPN*, 20 Apr. 2001, espn.com. Accessed 28 Feb. 2019.

5. Garrity, "Tiger Woods Wins the 2000 US Open at Pebble Beach by 15 Strokes."

6. "Woods Grabs Piece of History at Augusta."

7. "Woods Grabs Piece of History at Augusta."

8. Doug Williams. "How Tiger Woods, in His Heyday, Made Golf Cool by Transcending It." *ESPN*, 28 Mar. 2017, espn.com. Accessed 28 Feb. 2019.

9. Williams, "How Tiger Woods, in His Heyday, Made Golf Cool by Transcending It."

10. Chad Rau. "The Determinants of Attendance at PGA and PGA Tour Tournaments." *Colorado College*, May 2009, digitalccbeta.coloradocollege.edu. Accessed 28 Feb. 2019.

11. "Measuring the 'Tiger Effect'—Doubling of Tour Prizes, Billions into Players' Pockets." *SJA*, 6 Aug. 2014. sportingintelligence.com. Accessed 28 Feb. 2019.

12. Bob Martin. "Grand Stand." *Golf*, 19 Aug. 2011, golf.com. Accessed 28 Feb. 2019.

CHAPTER 6. HUSBAND, FATHER, CHAMPION

1. "Wood Blazes Competition at PGA Championship to Win 13th Major." *ESPN*, 13 Aug. 2007, espn.com. Accessed 28 Feb. 2019.

2. Bridget Harrison. "Tiger's Love Link—Golf Great Takes Bride in Posh Barbados Nuptials." *New York Post*, 6 Oct. 2004, nypost.com. Accessed 28 Feb. 2019.

3. "Woods Marries His Swedish Fiancée." *CNN*, 6 Oct. 2004, cnn.com. Accessed 28 Feb. 2019.

4. Frank Litsky. "Earl Woods, 74, Father of Tiger Woods, Dies." *New York Times*, 4 May 2006, nytimes.com. Accessed 28 Feb. 2019.

5. Doug Ferguson. "Earl Woods, Father of Tiger Woods, Dies." *Washington Post*, 3 May 2006, washingtonpost.com. Accessed 28 Feb. 2019.

6. Bob Harig. "How Tiger Woods Limped His Way to Improbable 2008 US Open Win." *ESPN*, 11 June 2018, espn.com. Accessed 28 Feb. 2019.

7. Bob Harig. "A Year Later, It's Time to Reminisce." *ESPN*, 14 June 2009, espn.com. Accessed 28 Feb. 2019.

8. Harig, "A Year Later, It's Time to Reminisce."

9. Tom Callahan. "The Class of '97." *Golf Digest*, 26 Mar. 2017, golfdigest.com. Accessed 28 Feb. 2019.

10. Harig, "A Year Later, It's Time to Reminisce."

11. Harig, "A Year Later, It's Time to Reminisce."

12. Tod Leonard. "The 52: Woods Legs Out Win in 2008 US Open." *San Diego Union-Tribune*, 9 Dec. 2016, sandiegouniontribune.com. Accessed 28 Feb. 2019.

13. Alan Shipnuck. "Tiger's 40 Biggest Moments: No. 3—The 2008 US Open." *Golf*, 28 Dec. 2015, golf.com. Accessed 28 Feb. 2019.

CHAPTER 7. THE FALL

1. Maureen Callahan. "The Night Tiger Woods Was Exposed as a Serial Cheater." *New York Post*, 24 Nov. 2013, nypost.com. Accessed 28 Feb. 2019.

2. Ian O'Connor. "After Yang Took Down Tiger, Major Golf Was Never the Same." *ESPN*, 11 Aug. 2015, espn.com. Accessed 28 Feb. 2019.

3. Callahan, "The Night Tiger Woods Was Exposed as a Serial Cheater."

4. Lee Ferran, et al. "Tiger Woods' Reputed Lover Rachel Uchitel: 'Tiger and I Are Not Friends.'" *ABC News*, 1 Dec. 2009, abcnews.go.com. Accessed 28 Feb. 2019.

5. Dan Gilgoff. "Tiger Woods' Apology Brings New Attention to Buddhism." *CNN*, 19 Feb. 2010, cnn.com. Accessed 28 Feb. 2019.

6. Gary Van Sickle. "Tiger's 40 Biggest Moments: No. 4—The 2009 Sex Scandal." *Golf*, 27 Dec. 2015, golf.com. Accessed 28 Feb. 2019.

7. "Tiger Woods." *PGA Tour*, n.d., pgatour.com. Accessed 28 Feb. 2019.

8. "Haney Discusses Leaving Woods." *ESPN*, 19 July 2010, espn.com. Accessed 28 Feb. 2019.

9. Well Wei. "Tiger Woods Lost $22 Million in Endorsements in 2010." *Business Insider*, 21 July 2010, businessinsider.com. Accessed 28 Feb. 2019.

10. Matthew Weaver. "Nike Stands by Sponsorship of Tiger Woods Despite 'Indiscretions.'" *Guardian*, 14 Dec. 2009, theguardian.com. Accessed 28 Feb. 2019.

11. "Gatorade Cuts Ties with Woods." *ESPN*, 27 Feb. 2010, espn.com. Accessed 28 Feb. 2019.

12. Randall Mell. "End of the Tiger Woods Era." *Golf Channel*, 27 Oct. 2010, golfchannel.com. Accessed 28 Feb. 2019.

13. Catherine Donaldson-Evans. "Tiger Woods Surprised, Gratified by Fans' Reaction." *People*, 23 Apr. 2010, people.com. Accessed 28 Feb. 2019.

CHAPTER 8. TRYING TO BOUNCE BACK

1. "Tiger Woods Wins at Bay Hill." *ESPN*, 26 Mar. 2012, espn.com. Accessed 28 Feb. 2019.

2. "Tiger Woods Wins at Bay Hill."

3. Bob Harig. "Tiger Woods Withdraws from WGC." *ESPN*, 12 Mar. 2012, espn.com. Accessed 28 Feb. 2019.

4. Bob Harig. "One of the Constants of Tiger Woods' Road Back to the Course: Caddie Joe LaCava." *ESPN*, 16 Mar. 2018, espn.com. Accessed 28 Feb. 2019.

5. Julie Mazziotta. "How Tiger Woods Got Back to Winning after 4 Surgeries to Fix His Severe Back Pain." *People*, 24 Sept. 2018, people.com. Accessed 28 Feb. 2019.

6. Steve Helling. "Tiger Woods and Ex-Wife Elin Nordegren 'Get Along Really Well' 9 Years after Scandal, Source Says." *People*, 8 Apr. 2018, people.com. Accessed 28 Feb. 2019.

7. Doug Ferguson. "Tiger Woods Ready to Roar in 2018 after Impressive Hero World Challenge Comeback." *Stuff*, 5 Dec. 2017, stuff.co.nz. Accessed 28 Feb. 2019.

8. Rex Hoggard. "Woods, Foley Share Blame in Tiger's Troubles." *Golf Channel*, 25 Aug. 2014, golfchannel.com. Accessed 28 Feb. 2019.

9. "How Tiger Hit 129 MPH Swing Speed—Fastest on Tour in 2018." *PGA*, 13 Mar. 2018, pga.com. Accessed 28 Feb. 2019.

10. Charles Curtis. "One Tiger Woods Stat Shows How Incredible His Comeback Is." *USA Today*, 15 Mar. 2018, ftw.usatoday.com. Accessed 28 Feb. 2019.

11. "James Lawton: Rory and Tiger May Be Able to Create Golf's Latest Great Rivalry." *Independent*, 2 Apr. 2012, independent.co.uk. Accessed 28 Feb. 2019.

12. David Magee. "Tiger Tracker, PGA Live Leaderboard: Tiger Woods Winning the Tour Championship 2018 So Far." *Newsweek*, 23 Sept. 2018, newsweek.com. Accessed 28 Feb. 2019.

13. Bob Harig. "Tiger Woods Caps Comeback by Winning Tour Championship." *ESPN*, 24 Sept. 2018, espn.com. Accessed 28 Feb. 2019.

14. Harig, "Tiger Woods Caps Comeback by Winning Tour Championship."

15. "Tiger Woods 'Proud' of Season as He Eyes $10M FedEx Cup Bonus." *Fox43*, 20 Sept. 2018, fox43.com. Accessed 28 Feb. 2019.

16. Michael Bamberger. "Ever Doubt Him? Tiger Woods Caps Once-Unthinkable Comeback with Dominant Win at Tour Championship." *Golf*, 23 Sept. 2018, golf.com. Accessed 28 Feb. 2019.

CHAPTER 9. LEGACY

1. Bob Gillespie. "How Tiger's Masters Win Changed the Face of Golf." *PGA*, 7 Feb. 2018, pga.com. Accessed 28 Feb. 2019.

2. Gillespie, "How Tiger's Masters Win Changed the Face of Golf."

3. Michael Weinreb. "'He Didn't Fit the Mold of a Revolutionary.'" *Ringer*, 6 Apr. 2017, theringer.com. Accessed 28 Feb. 2019.

4. Bob Harig. "How Much Has Tiger's First Masters Win Influenced the Sport?" *ESPN*, 31 Mar. 2017, espn.com. Accessed 28 Feb. 2019.

5. Avis Thomas-Lester. "Blacks Break into the Swing of Golf." *Washington Post*, 17 Aug. 2000, washingtonpost.com. Accessed 28 Feb. 2019.

6. Matt Brennan. "What Happens to Golf after Tiger?" *Deadspin*, 14 Aug. 2014, deadspin.com. Accessed 28 Feb. 2019.

7. Michael A. Fletcher. "Even at HBCUs, Black Golfers are in the Minority." *Undefeated*, 5 Apr. 2018, theundefeated.com. Accessed 28 Feb. 2019.

8. Simon Caney. "Rory Credits Tiger Woods for Inspiring Him." *Your Golf Travel*, 7 Apr. 2015, yourgolftravel.com. Accessed 28 Feb. 2019.

9. Doug Williams. "How Tiger Woods, in His Heyday, Made Golf Cool by Transcending It." *ESPN*, 28 Mar. 2017, espn.com. Accessed 28 Feb. 2019.

10. Agence France-Presse. "Proud Tiger Woods Keeps Open Mind about Golf Career ahead of 40th Birthday." *National*, 29 Dec. 2015, thenational.ae. Accessed 28 Feb. 2019.

11. "Tiger Woods, and How Leaders Lose Their Edge." *Phil Cooke*, n.d., philcooke.com. Accessed 28 Feb. 2019.

12. "Tiger Woods on His Comeback and His One Regret." *CBS News*, 20 Oct. 2016, cbsnews.com. Accessed 28 Feb. 2019.

13. Iain Strachan. "Rory McIlroy Labels Tiger Woods 'Greatest Player Ever.'" *Sporting News*, 7 Sept. 2016, sportingnews.com. Accessed 28 Feb. 2019.

14. Bob Harig. "Debating Tiger's Legacy." *ESPN*, 30 Dec. 2016, espn.com. Accessed 28 Feb. 2019.

INDEX

ABOUT THE AUTHOR

Doug Williams is a freelance writer and former newspaper reporter and editor. This is his twelfth book about sports. He and his wife live in San Diego, California, where they enjoy spending time with family, hiking, traveling, and reading. He was the golf editor for the *San Diego Union-Tribune* for many years, including 2008 when Tiger Woods won the US Open championship in a playoff at Torrey Pines in San Diego.